INNOVATION AND ENTREPRENEURSHIP SPACE

DR.KIRAN KUMARI PATIL

First Published in February 2023

ISBN: 978-93-5704-548-3

BLUEROSE PUBLISHERS
www.BlueRoseONE.com
info@bluerosepublishers.com
+91 8882 898 898

Cover Design:
Aman Sharma

Typographic Design:
Namrata Saini

Distributed by: BlueRose, Amazon, Flipkart

Acknowledgment

I would like to express my heartfelt gratitude to the many people who have made this book a reality. First and foremost, I would like to thank my family for their unwavering support and encouragement throughout this journey. You have been my rock and I could not have done this without you.

I would also like to thank Honourable Chancellor of REVA University for his encouragement and support. I thank my friends and colleagues and LG soft for their invaluable feedback and advice, which have helped me to shape this book into what it is today. Your insights and perspectives have been truly invaluable and I am so grateful for your support.

I am also indebted to the many experts in the field who have generously shared their knowledge and expertise with me. Your guidance has been essential to the success of this book and I could not have done it without you.

Finally, I would like to thank my publisher and the many editors, designers, and other professionals who have worked tirelessly to bring this book to life. Your dedication and hard work have been truly inspiring and I am honored to have had the opportunity to work with such an amazing team.

Thank you all for your unwavering support, encouragement, and belief in this book. I am deeply grateful for each and every one of you.

Contents

Academia to Entrepreneurship 1

Creativity, Innovation and Entrepreneurship prime focus for holistic education: New National Education Policy 2020 9

Essentials to Convert an IDEA into Reality 16

Entrepreneurship education for budding minds 20

Role of Emotional Intelligence in Entrepreneurial Journey .. 26

Technology adoption is only path to sustained growth for SMEs 30

Start-Up Funding Challenges and Types 35

All about Start-up IDEAS: Essential Steps to Evaluating Yourself & Business Idea 41

Intellectual Property Rights, critical for the success of startups 47

Women Entrepreneurs for Building Strong Economy 53

National start-up Day and its Significance 59

Academia to Entrepreneurship

"Academic and Entrepreneurship go hand-in-hand"

A foot in two worlds

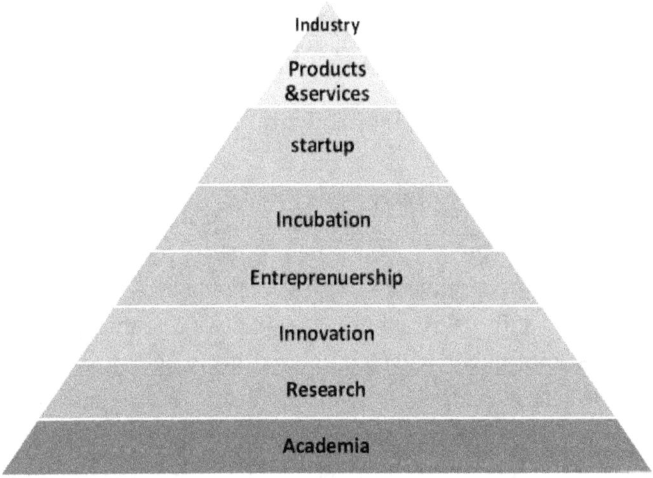

Industry

Products &services

startup

Incubation

Entreprenuership

Innovation

Research

Academia

Figure 1.0: 8 Layered Model, RAY Model

There are several barriers to academic entrepreneurship. First, academic entrepreneurs must possess a rare blend of skills. They must have the attributes of traditional scientists, including inner drive, rigor, and technical skills. They must also possess the attributes of traditional entrepreneurs, such as the ability to recognize business opportunities and create value for the customer, and the willingness to take risks. Academic entrepreneurs must be able to aim high while delivering on their promises and discerning which research endeavors are most likely to contribute to the bottom line.

Traditional science education doesn't embrace entrepreneurship, so many young scientists feel unqualified. Principal investigators often take the view that Ph.D. students and postdocs should focus entirely on research. Another disincentive is that, in too many departments, patents and startup companies may count for little during hiring and promotion.

Even in a supportive environment, the challenges of doing both at once—becoming a world-class researcher and commercializing a technology—are so formidable that many early-career scientists come to see them as insurmountable.

Finding entrepreneurial inspiration in an academic environment

Let's consider some inspiring facts. The number of patents, licenses, and spin-off companies created by academics is increasing. According to a study published in 2009 by researchers at the Massachusetts Institute of Technology (MIT) Sloan School of Management, alumni from MIT **had created 25,800 active companies** with worldwide annual sales of $2 trillion. These days, many universities support budding academic entrepreneurs through ad-hoc courses and access to technology transfer offices, business incubators, and innovation parks.

One such ecosystem is created at REVA University Bangalore by the name REVA – NEST a Technology Business incubator and start-up on campus. We at REVA – NEST developed an 8-Layered model called as RAY Model for establishing startups and connecting to the industry in the academic environment, as shown in figure 1.0. According to RAY Model, academics is the foundation for research. With suitable research, it is possible to develop innovative ideas. In the fourth stage with exposure to the entrepreneurship world, one can start their venture as a start-up and deliver products and services as per the market needs. Going ahead one can establish an Industry and become a successful Techno-entrepreneur. RAY model is a systematic approach to establish industry in the academic ecosystem. The study shows that academia and entrepreneurship goes hand -in -hand.

An Innovative Low-Cost Respiratory Device – Jeeva Setu 2.0 Designed and Developed by REVA University R&D and Technology Business Incubation team

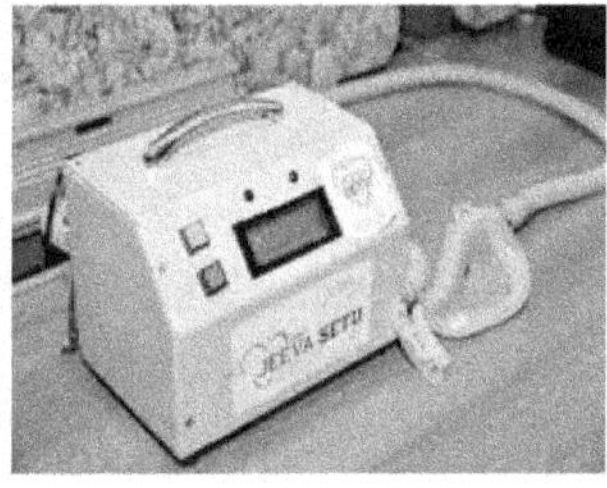

A research team from the School of Computer and Information technology and School of Electronics and communication has designed and developed a low cost non-invasive, blower-based ventilator for use in emergency pandemic situations and resource-poor environments. This innovative device is a pressure support ventilator (PSV) which adjusts the pressure on the fly as the patient breathes, eliminating the frequent need for a human operator. It includes an assistive control system (ACS) that uses triggering so that if the patient makes an effort to breathe, it helps them and if not, it maintains the set pressure. The device measures flow rate and vital parameters like pulse rate, oxygen levels, respiratory rate, body can be measured and monitored by the doctors or family members remotely through a cloud-based web application. The device has been tested at the healthcare center by authorized medical team. Work has been patented and published. The device is under the process of regulatory approval. The team is open to collaborating with Industry, academia, startup experts to reach to end customers. This device can be deployed at all rural primary healthcare centers. Device needs no special medical technician to operate, cost-effective, and easy to operate.

Business Sustainability through Collaboration and Partnership

Doing everything by yourself can be tempting in the beginning when funds are few and ambitions high. While there's nothing wrong with a hands-on approach, taking on more than you can handle, especially in areas where you lack experience, can be damaging. Sustainable growth is among the biggest challenges any business leader faces, but it isn't a problem if we find right partners to collaborate with.

Collaboration is one of the keys for unlocking sustainability. No single organization or sector has the knowledge or resources to "go it alone." Leaders from all sectors of society agree that solving sustainability challenges will require unparalleled cooperation. This report is a comprehensive review of what we know about partnering for sustainability. **Many companies are actively** integrating sustainability principles into their businesses, according to a recent McKinsey survey

Sustainability is "the primary moral and economic imperative of the 21st century," according to Mervyn King. It is also considered to be "one of the most important sources of both opportunities and risks for businesses".

Business collaboration benefits

Key benefits of business collaboration fall under several categories:

- **Financial benefits** - for example, the ability to boost domestic or export sales, to tender for larger contracts or cut costs by sharing resources.

- **Human capital** - for example, the ability to develop employees' skills and capabilities, safeguard jobs, increase employment and encourage staff motivation.

- **Physical capital** - for example, the ability to share facilities, resources, equipment and raw materials.

- **Intellectual capital** - for example, the ability to tap into combined expertise, knowledge and capabilities.

Types of business collaboration

Collaborative networking can take many forms. From strategic alliances and partnerships to business networks, development networks or even regional and national collaboration

Business networks

These involve businesses working together for **specific purposes** where the collaboration has identifiable and measurable benefits to all participants in the network. Key features of a business network are:

- A Group Of Businesses As The Core (Although Members May Include Academia And Other Organizations)
- A Restricted Membership
- Agreed Co-Operation Between Members
- Common Business Objectives Likely To Boost Mutual Competitiveness And Financial Gain

Development network

These are the most basic forms of networks consisting simply of businesses associating with other businesses. Their activity is often confined to:

- Networking
- The Exchange Of Information
- Shared Services

These networks are usually informal and unstructured. They are also less likely to have a purpose linked directly to financial gain or competitive advantage for the members.

Regional business network

These are geographically defined groups of companies, educational institutions, local councils, and economic development agencies connected by linkages across sectors. They can make up business clusters that share a common regional location, where 'region' is defined as:

- A Geographical Area
- A Labour Market
- An Economic Unit

Regional networks often bring benefits to businesses but this is not always their sole purpose.

Successful business collaboration

Some common elements make collaborative networking success more likely. For example:

- Mutuality And Solidarity - working together for the benefit of each other
- Information Exchange - communicating openly about problems and ways of working

Businesses that collaborate may also find it helpful to have a similar culture, operational synergies and a desire to make collaboration work. Support from top management and key people within a business will also contribute to successful collaboration.

Stages of business collaboration

Collaborative networks are often achieved in stages involving:

- **Exploration** - looking at the potential benefits and ways of collaborating
- **Assimilation** - transforming the ideas into a working collaboration
- **Exploitation** - pooling resources and knowledge to create new processes or products

Challenges can emerge at each stage of this life cycle

Planning for collaboration

A foundation of any collaboration is establishing:

- A Clear Purpose
- An Agreed Business Opportunity
- Clear Rules Of Engagement Between Members

This will allow you to set clear expectations regarding the inputs and outputs of members. It will also enable you to align the interests of the initial membership. Once you define the focus of the network, you can assess and design the criteria for additional members to bring the greatest benefit.

Partnership

Here we have a few recommendations pertaining to all partners' selection in general:

- Adopt a problem-centric rather than a firm-centric model of stakeholders.
- Frame the partnership as a learning process.
- Construct fair processes and manage conflicts.
- Don't expect to come up with a quick solution.
- Ensure voice for all participants.
- Set evaluation criteria.
- Allow time for representatives' constituencies to review and ratify agreements.

Creativity, Innovation and Entrepreneurship prime focus for holistic education: New National Education Policy 2020

The Union Cabinet approved The National Education Policy 2020-NEP on July 29, 2020[1]. The NEP proposes a paradigm shift on how education is disbursed by various institutions across the country. As the present education system limits itself in various aspects and unable to encourage innovative and out-of-the-box thinking among young minds. A much needed move for the transformation of education ecosystem The NEP seeks to establish an educational landscape that caters to the overall-development of students in order to create industry ready work force to meet global industry requirements and also emphasis on entrepreneurship and startups ecosystem. This work presents NEP 2020 from creativity, innovation and entrepreneurship perspective.

Introduction:

Creativity, innovation and entrepreneurship remain at the heart of the Policy. The Ministry of Human Resource Development (now, the Ministry of Education) has recognized that India lags behind when it comes to research, innovation and entrepreneurship. This lack of creative and critical thinking mainly stems from the fact that the current educational framework does not award such thinking. This has resulted in stagnation of Intellectual properties, local manufacturing and self-sustainability. Creativity leads to innovation and innovation eventually results in the generation of Intellectual Property and further can be taken up to entrepreneurship and startups.

New Policy aims for Universalization of Education from pre-school to secondary level with 100 % GER in school education by 2030 and aims to bring 2 crore out of school children back into the main stream [5]. New Policy aims for Universalization of Education from pre-school to secondary level with 100 % GER in school education by 2030

Key Principles of NEP 2020

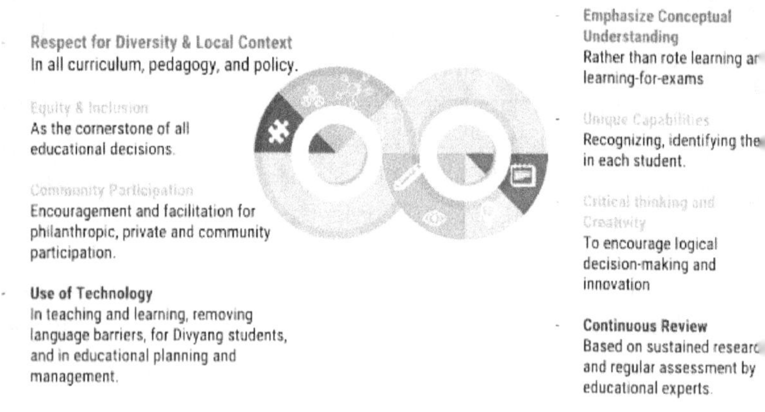

A multi-disciplinary approach to develop 21ˢᵗ century skills

A multi-disciplinary approach that eases the divide between arts, science and technical colleges is a welcome move to prepare students for jobs in the future. In the longer run, the NEP aims to make education flexible and broad-based to develop equivalence of vocational and academic streams. The purpose is to create useful capabilities while offering specializations across disciplines.

The focus of the framework is to allow students flexibility to select a field of study that aligns with their area of interest. For example, a student pursuing music will be able to learn coding and science together. The result will be a creative combination as well as a flexible curriculum for students.

More importantly, NEP signals the end of rote learning. The comprehensive framework brings in assessments based on the application of core concepts to inculcate a problem-solving mindset. The focus will be on revamping the curricula in tandem with global standards. Integrating vocational and academic courses will help develop industry-ready professionals, equipped with '21st-century skills'.

With the introduction of many transformational reforms, the NEP will undoubtedly result in an increased generation of ideas leading to an increase SMEs and MSMEs in the future.

The policy envisions a holistic education by bringing an integration of sciences, social sciences, arts, humanities, and sports to actualize multidisciplinary culture in academia. Conceptual understanding, creativity, and critical thinking will be the foundation of research and innovation in the new vision. It is aimed at producing revolutionary research and preventing the reproduction of similar works lacking pioneering prospects. The policy also envisions the transformation of India into an equitable and vibrant knowledge society by providing high-quality education to all. The 'demographic dividend' of India can be fully utilized by inspiring and encouraging a considerable number of committed scholars to quality research in various fields. The policy also aims to build a holistic approach to the preparation of professionals by ensuring broad-based competencies, an understanding of the social-human context, and a strong ethical compass, in addition to the highest quality professional capacities.

The Proliferation of Intellectual Property:

1. Establishment of the National Research Foundation (NRF).
2. The abolishment of Rote Learning
3. Streamlining PhDs and Degrees with Research
4. Fueling Research and Innovation in Colleges and Universities
5. Education 4.0 and the National Education Technology Forum
6. Disruptive Technologies

Preparing a roadmap for entrepreneurship

Given the rapid pace of technological development combined with sheer creativity, the NEP encourages student entrepreneurs to pursue vocational education in collaboration with industry and in accordance with Sustainable Development Goal 4.4 (SDG) [2]. Integration of vocational education with educational offerings in all institutions by choosing focus areas based on skills gap analysis and mapping of local opportunities will develop entrepreneurial competencies in addition to capacities and will go a long way toward making vocational education a part of the larger vision of holistic education.

Framework for 21ˢᵗ Century Learning and Era of specializations

NEP 2020 will ensure the holistic development of learners. We have to advance our students with 21st-century skills. These 21st Century skills will be: Critical Thinking, Creativity, Collaboration, Curiosity, and Communication. The new NEP is a means of fulfilling New India, New Expectations, and New Requirements. NEP will bring in a reduction in curriculum content to enhance essential learning and critical thinking. Stress will also be given to removing language barriers in order to achieve better results in learning.

Further, as part of a holistic education, the ideas of imaginative and flexible curricular structures enable creative combinations of disciplines for study. NEP provides for rigorous research-based specialization by giving opportunities for multi-disciplinary work including industry; opportunities for internships with local industry/businesses-houses; actively engaging with the practical side of learning, all of which are bound give impetus to entrepreneurship.

Focus on technical education for the overall growth and development

Also, the focus on technical education is decisive for India's overall growth and development and is well addressed in NEP. The technical sectors like engineering, technology, management, architecture, town planning, pharmacy, hotel management, and catering technology continue to demand well-qualified individuals, and hence closer collaboration between industry and institutions to drive innovation and research is actively encouraged in NEP [3].

Soliciting inputs from national and international entrepreneurs and practitioners; integrating vocational education programs into mainstream education, complementing with a parallel voluntary and more business-focused approach; creating entrepreneurship-oriented programs with expanded high-quality opportunities that can make effective use of these qualifications would allow breakthroughs to be brought into NEP and/or implementation in an optimal fashion. Besides, as part of multi-disciplinary education, the focus will be on research & innovation by setting up start-up incubation centers, technology development centers, centers in frontier areas of research, and greater industry-academic linkages. These initiatives will go a long way in preserving and promoting entrepreneurial acumen and will also vastly strengthen the existing entrepreneurial sector.

The idea of infusing entrepreneurship into education has spurred much enthusiasm in the past few decades. A myriad of effects has been stated to result from this, such as economic growth, job creation, and increased societal resilience, but also individual growth, increased engagement and improved equality. Putting this idea into practice will however, pose significant challenges alongside the stated positive effects.

However, the NEP provides a novel path to the education system so as to make India a global knowledge power and economic giant.

The way forward – NEP 2020

In a nutshell, NEP aims to usher in producing prolific, productive, and contributing young minds for building an inclusive, equitable, and self-reliant Nation. The New National Education Policy NEP promotes a participatory, holistic, and inclusive approach to education. The policy released is the result of field experiences, factual research, feedback from stakeholders, and lessons learned from best practices. Its progressive march is a shift to a more scientific approach to education.

The authorized structure caters to the cognitive development of the child, and gives them social and physical awareness emphasizing on creativity. The new structure can make Nation become one of the leading countries in the world and make our children and youth realize their potential and contribute to national development.

Essentials to Convert an IDEA into Reality

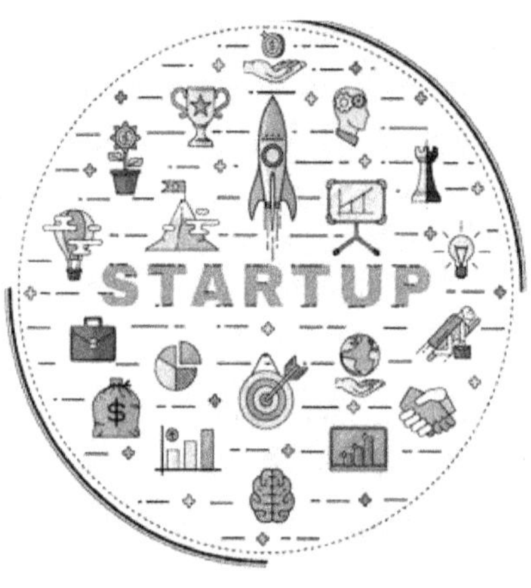

For an aspiring entrepreneurs, it is often common to come up with a variety of crazy ideas for new businesses without much clarity on implementation and how to convert an idea into a business venture. We can think of a business concept as a bridge between an idea and a business plan. Basically, it focuses on one's thinking so that the entrepreneur can identify the opportunities and challenges of his/her proposed venture. Converting an idea into a business concept requires thinking about how the product or service will be sold and the targeted customers, the USP's of the product or service.

Preparing a written concept statement helps unearth critical components of a venture and begins research into key factors that may be more thoroughly addressed in a business plan. As the business idea takes the form of a concept statement, the entrepreneur can evaluate the business more effectively for potential challenges and pitfalls.

Following few fundamental steps to be considered to convert your idea into a start-up:

Complete Market Research.

It is a common tendency that most of the people to skip this first step and chase ideas without really evaluating their monetary and technological worth. It is absolutely essential to the success of your start-up o begin by defining a problem and seeing if the end solution is actually something that customer needs.

Define your Unique Sales Proposition.

What exactly will you be offering? Is it a product, is it a service, what are the particulars of your product or service and how are they different from the rest of your competitors? Answering these questions will help you put your idea into concrete and saleable terms.

Setting Up a Legal Entity, a Company.

This is important espccially when you want to be taken seriously by investors and clients. When you register your company and incorporate, you are essentially turning your business into a legal entity which helps you decide the structure and be prepared to collaborate with investors at an appropriate time.

An effective and Clear Business Plan is the Key.

Business plans are important documents used to attract investment before a company has established a proven track record. They are also a good way for companies to keep themselves on target going forward. Note down what you want to accomplish with your new business, chalk out goals and milestones, and a step-by-step road map to get you where you need to be to make your start-up profitable.

Start Building Talented Team.

A talent pool is must, one person may not have all the skills required to run the start-up-and neither should they! Real businesses delegate specialized assignments like accounting, tech development, and product development to professionals who are seasoned in this area. In order to be successful in converting ideas into a start-up, start on-boarding talented professionals who share the same values from the get-go.

Get Associated with an Accelerator or an Incubator.

Collaboration is essential to explore and knowledge sharing for beginners. In case shortage of funds to invest as many start-ups are, a great way to access additional resources and expertise is to join an incubator that helps businesses by helping them tap into a network of experts, investments as well as training to hone skills required.

Validate the Prototype – Market Fit Test.

Now it's time to test product on the market! Validating your idea on a small scale can allow you to test real-time market response with minimum resources and funds investment. These above steps considered and followed diligently you will likely to have a viable, user-tested, sellable product that meets a specific market demand.

Plan Low Cost Marketing Strategies for your Business.

Determining how to promote your business can be an ongoing challenge. If your business is new, you may not know how to advertise your business to get your name known. You need proven advertising and marketing tactics to find new customers without spending a fortune. These need to include a mix of traditional and digital marketing. To market your business successfully you need a planned, organized approach. Hit or miss marketing wastes time and money. Start by defining your marketing strategy and setting a budget, Identify your best prospects, and then determine the best promotional strategies to reach them. Be as specific as possible. Online and offline marketing methods work hand-in-hand to bring in customers and clients and keep them coming back. In the era of Internet of things, digital marketing isn't an option—it's a necessity.

Entrepreneurship education for budding minds

In the present economic situation, having knowledge of an academic subject is no longer sufficient for a new graduate. Students are increasingly required to have skills and abilities which will increase their employability, such as the retrieval and handling of information; communication and presentation; planning and problem solving; and social development and interaction. Entrepreneurial education and training provide individuals with the ability to recognize commercial opportunities, self-esteem, knowledge, and skills to act on them. It includes instruction in opportunity recognition, commercializing a concept, managing resources, and initiating a business venture. It also includes instruction in traditional business disciplines such as management, marketing, information systems and finance. Entrepreneurs or the move towards self-employment is, and will continue to become, an increasingly important element of economic growth and development. It is essential to have the infrastructure required to facilitate an entrepreneurial mind-set and encourage self-employment. Having a culture of the creation of a new enterprise is a critical aspect of this infrastructure, as it will encourage students to take the risk of starting a business. Entrepreneurship education does not just benefit those entering the fields of science, technology, and business. Students interested in the arts, social sciences, and similar fields can also develop their imagination and learn how to apply creative thinking skills to real-world problems.

The significance of entrepreneurship education in primary & secondary education will develop an entrepreneurial mind-set among young minds. It is now emerging as one of the fastest growing fields across the globe, for bringing a positive impact on economic growth and employment opportunities. Entrepreneurship education should start from an early age, advancing gradually through all levels of education, to inculcate a process of lifelong learning in students. Realizing the need, the draft National Education Policy 2019 (NEP) of India has outlined some special steps that need to be taken to incorporate it in the School curriculum.

Empowering students by teaching entrepreneurship at school:

1. Prepare your students to face and overcome uncertainty

The recent COVID-19 pandemic has taught all of us an important lesson: Our lives can dramatically change at any time. Some economic experts predicted many people's jobs would become automated during the next few decades, even before the global pandemic. Teachers can't always predict exactly what students will need to know after they graduate. Still, teaching entrepreneurship skills can help students handle, and sometimes even welcome, the changes happening in technology, business, and society in general. These skills include problem-solving, teamwork, and empathy, as well as learning to accept failure as a part of the growth process.

2. Students develop their creativity and collaboration skills

Creativity, innovation, and collaboration are integral elements of entrepreneurship. These skills are highly valued by the top colleges and most businesses in the world and will be used by your students well beyond their middle school and high school years. Entrepreneurship education fosters advanced skills of creativity and innovative thinking which empowers and inspires students to take initiative, risk decisions, and accept responsibility to thrive in the challenging world. Such students develop the ability to recognize opportunities, thinks critically, solve problem creatively, and above all learn to push boundaries. The skills of critical-thinking, communication, and collaboration not only help in making them forward-thinking individuals or develop in them a nimbleness to adapt to rapid change but also in shaping their own careers.

Collaboration and working within a team allow students to become aware of different ways of critical thinking, develop effective communication skills, and identify the strengths and roles of themselves and their teammates. Creativity is required when faced with the important responsibility of negotiating differences in opinions, ideas, and personalities among the team. Without this essential executive function, a company would either fail to realize each individual's full potential or likely, fail altogether. Most start-ups fail based on teaming issues, and anyone who has worked in a company knows the importance of good leadership and teamwork. Within a start-up, where everyone coming together has a lot of experience and previous leadership experience, there is no specified leader. Everyone has the propensity for leadership, and everyone must find ways to trust each other, collaborate, communicate, and cooperate. All it takes is one person undermining the collaborative spirit to make for a poor dynamic, and all it can take is one person to help rectify it through great leadership.

3. Learning to identify and recognize problems at an early age builds confidence

Before learning how to address problems, students must first learn how to recognize them. Problem-solving exercises have long been a part of traditional schooling. The same cannot be said for detecting difficulties. Traditionally, problem-solving is taught by presenting students with issues that are already clearly defined by someone else. In the real world, problems can only be solved when they have been properly identified and described. Entrepreneurship education helps children learn how to identify problems they have never dealt with before. This skill is much needed now and will continue to be needed in the future.

4. Handhold students become resilient

Becoming an entrepreneur is an ongoing journey filled with lots of ups and downs, even when the economy is thriving. Teaching entrepreneurship encourages students to figure out their passions and how to be persistent when pursuing their interests. Students also learn how to stick with a business idea, or similar project, especially when times are tough. Learning how to work through problems and adapt to changes improves a student's chances of having professional and personal success long after they leave your classroom.

Integrating entrepreneurship into the curriculum develops knowledge, skills, and attitudes in students that impact academic performance and develop entrepreneurial competency. It helps them to identify and hone their latent talents as well as act in a socially responsible way. Students develop the skill to deliberate, identify potential audiences, seek approval from people, understand their need and learn how to sell their ideas. They also learn the importance of research and understand the importance of learning from one's mistakes. Education plays a significant role in the growth and development of a nation and the economic growth of a nation is supported by the entrepreneurial thinking skills and activities of its people. They are the driving force which fuel economic growth. Entrepreneurial innovations with technological advancements and global competitiveness are essential for a state or a country to create new jobs and aid in economy growth.

It is very important to coach kids on how to deal with failure efficiently, and entrepreneurship education does offer the necessary exposure to handle failures and learn from one's mistakes in one journey to success. At times, letting students learn from failures can be a good thing for healthy growth not only in entrepreneurship but also in life.

Developing knowledge on entrepreneurship need not make a person an entrepreneur, but it will definitely nurture an enterprising mindset that leads one towards excellence in school and beyond the school years. Similarly, entrepreneurship is not confined to economic activities and the creation of start-ups, it embraces other areas of life, like stimulating students to think creatively and aspiringly.

Entrepreneurship education shapes young minds to master the skills of the future. With an uncertain future ahead owing to numerous reasons such as technological advancements and population growth, entrepreneurship can be seen as a significant career option among the current generation.

Role of Emotional Intelligence in Entrepreneurial Journey

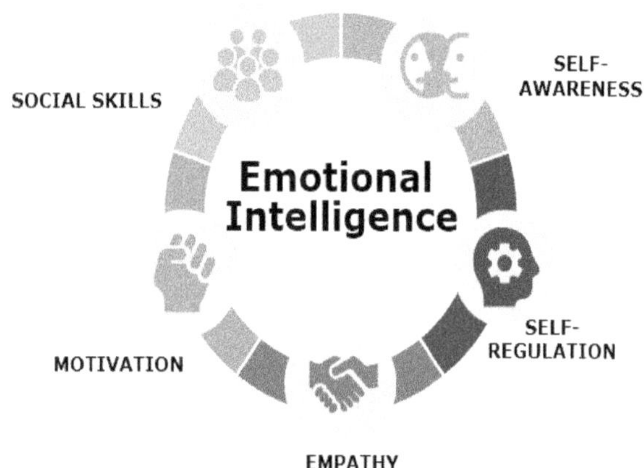

Emotional intelligence, in a nutshell, is the skill of detecting and understanding emotions in others as well as oneself. Emotional intelligent people are generally good at managing their own emotions and helping others manage theirs.

Emotionally intelligent people are good at putting themselves in someone else's shoes and seeing challenges from different perspectives, which can also help them solve problems for their team and clients. Entrepreneurship requires to of maturity in understanding things from others perspective and most of times it is proved that Emotional Intelligence plays a key role to success as an entrepreneur.

Entrepreneurs need to be self-driven and motivated individuals. Business is about relationships, and Emotional Intelligence is the number one skill needed for you to connect with your team and customers – and drive business success.

For an entrepreneur, mastering EQ skill can be the difference between success and failure. Those entrepreneurs who neglect to develop emotional intelligence tend to get stressed easily make more mistakes, and make reactive decisions leading to business damage.

Emotionally intelligent people are empathetic, such qualities typically make them excellent, respected communicators. Although the traditional workplace follows emotional intelligence on a priority, it can be extremely helpful—and even crucial—for the entrepreneurial journey too.

Various skills that make a person to have high emotionally intelligent and are essential for an Entrepreneur are:

1. Improved self-awareness

Understanding where do we stand emotionally can be very helpful as an entrepreneur. Being able to identify and healthfully express your own emotions is a strength. The ability to understand your own emotions and how they affect the people around can help you make better decisions.

2. More effective communication

Any Idea how well do we communicate with others? Studies suggest that our daily communication breakdown is as follows:

- 9 percent of writing
- 16 percent reading
- 30 percent speaking
- 45 percent listening

Unfortunately, a lot of people struggle with active listening because they are either talking over someone or are too consumed with what's going on in their own head to pay attention to what the other person is saying. As Peter Drucker says, ***"The most important thing in communication is to hear what isn't being said."*** Successful entrepreneurs who possess strong emotional intelligence value the importance of listening. They realize that, by allowing others to feel heard, it creates trust with people. Furthermore, it allows them to learn more about their audience.

It's difficult to have a deep conversation with someone if you don't empathize with them. If you can't identify with the emotions of others, communication is more difficult and less effective overall. Entrepreneurs with high emotional intelligence can leverage empathy, problem-solving, and social skills to come up with solutions, create strong relationships, and ultimately, win people over

3. Being Empathetic toward others

Empathy is looking at and understanding the concerns from others' perspectives. This quality will help in building trust among clients and that in turn creates strong relationships with people because they have a genuine interest and concern for their well-being. As a result, they are master influencers. People want to follow their work because they trust who they are as a person and what they stand for.

4. Better control over emotions

The journey of an Entrepreneur is not at all a walk in the park. One has to face many, roadblocks on the path to success, and entrepreneurs will have to deal with everything that comes on their way. Being able to control emotions is key when communicating with investors and other important stakeholders.

5. Open to Life Long Learning

Always seek constructive feedback from colleagues, mentors, coaches, peers, and team members for self-improvement. Weaknesses are only seen as opportunities to grow and become more. Being open to new and lifelong learning with a growth mindset will make the entrepreneurial journey smooth and safe.

In the words of Daniel Goleman himself, *"If your emotional abilities aren't in hand, if you don't have self-awareness, if you are not able to manage your distressing emotions, if you can't have empathy and have effective relationships, then no matter how smart you are, you are not going to get very far."*

The only way to develop emotional intelligence is by practicing it in action. Just like any skill that you want to master, it will require that you invest time, energy, hard work, and effort into it.

Higher emotional intelligence is a greater indicator of strong performance (whether that be in the workplace, in testing situations, and so on) than high IQ.

In terms of entrepreneurship, having high emotional intelligence is extremely beneficial. With high emotional intelligence comes a better understanding of the other's needs, feelings, and overall situation. As such, an entrepreneur with high emotional intelligence can better create a product or service to fit the needs of their target customer. Similarly, entrepreneurs with high emotional intelligence can better work with and understand their co-workers and clients, and cultivate better relationships with them as a result of their heightened sensitivity to the emotional states of those around them. Finally, emotionally intelligent entrepreneurs uses their understanding of the needs of others to be a better leader. When it comes to being a leader, they rely on empathy and understanding, not an iron fist.

Technology adoption is only path to sustained growth for SMEs

Technology adoption in SMEs context is a growing area of interest in developing countries. Technology adoption is also crucial for the growth of business in the private sector.

Especially during the Covid-19 pandemic, the majority of Indian SME's to shift online to scale up and succeed, with small business owners waking up to the need of technology as the only path for sustained growth. Small businesses don't necessarily have the resources to make large investments in technology but the disruption has made them realise how adopting to digital can help them take advantage of opportunities in today's changing environment. Even as MSMEs are struggling for survival, it is crucial to evaluate what the Government and technology companies can do to help small businesses carve out a growth path for themselves.

Information technology has transformed the social and business environment. Technology often deals with methods or tools used to gather, manipulate, store and communicate information. Emerging technology includes new or advanced hardware or software. Emerging technology is a sector of information technology responsible for developing new products or devices that are expected to be widely used in the next 5 to 10 years. Businesses often look to emerging technologies for new services or devices that will help them create a competitive business advantage. Emerging technology might also include advancements of technologies the business already uses. These advancements often allow companies to enhance business operations at a cheaper cost.

Increased Communication

Technology may improve how a company communicates, and various innovative communication methods are in the works. Virtual offices are an evolving communication technology in which people meet, discuss diverse issues, and execute corporate functions. Voice over Internet Protocol is a method of communicating via audio or video technology. These technologies enable businesses to collaborate with employees or other businesses all around the world.

Robotics and Artificial Intelligence

Two important emerging technology fields for businesses are robotics and artificial intelligence. Robotics is an engineering science and technology field that uses electronic or mechanical technology to replace human labor. Manufacturing and production firms currently use robots in their systems, and the robotics technology industry seeks to expand to other business industries. Artificial intelligence focuses on creating intelligent machines for businesses to use. Businesses use this technology by entering information into business machines that can develop the information and make accurate predictions and identify trends.

Research and Development

Emerging technology helps companies create more effective and less costly research and development processes. Photonic computing, quantum computing, biometrics and nanotechnology are a few technologies that allow companies to find new ways for researching and breaking down information and other business processes. These technologies are commonly used in the chemical, petroleum, medical and other industries. Increased research and development technologies can help companies develop products more efficiently and bring them to the consumer market faster than in previous years.

Impacts of Technology on Small Business

Small businesses rely on technology to help them operate on a daily basis. From laptop computers with Internet capabilities to printers, online file storage and Web-based applications, technological advances impact small businesses across various industries. Technology has the potential to affect small business in positive and adverse ways, depending on the goals a business has a in place, the products they chose to use, and how well entrepreneurs and their employees adapt to new systems.

Flexible Work Environments

Technology gives small business owners and their employees the option to work in the office, from home, on the road, and even from across the country. Affording small business owners the opportunity to hire talent from all over the world, technology can help businesses gain a competitive edge in the global environment.

Instant Connection with Customers

Small business owners no longer have to mail surveys to customers and wait for weeks for replies, nor do they have to call customers for feedback. Technology gives small businesses the ability to connect with their customers via e-mail, blogs, social networks, and forums. Small business owners can take advantage of this instant connection by getting feedback from customers and applying it to their businesses immediately if they see fit.

Online Stores

Technology allows small businesses like crafters, clothing, and accessories designers, and painters an option to set up online stores, rather than investing in costly outlets. With consumers migrating to the Internet to find everything from gifts to ordering groceries, the popularity of online shopping increases with the variety of products and services. Businesses with storefronts can create online stores to expand their visibility and reach target markets beyond their neighborhoods and surrounding communities.

Employee Training

As small businesses implement new technologies into their processes, they are tasked with providing training to new and veteran employees. While new employees are likely to easily adapt to the technologies, veteran employees may resist the new technologies or experience a learning curve, which may temporarily reduce productivity

Small and Medium Enterprises (SME's) are the driving force for the promotion of an economy. The impact of technology adoption is influential in improving the performance of SMEs. The improved perception of technology leads to the tendency toward usage behavior of innovation at the organizational level. Technology adoption behavior significantly improves organizational performance in terms of profit, growth, and market share of Indonesian SMEs.

Start-Up Funding Challenges and Types

Building your own company is exciting, but it can also be hard, and it requires investment, a lot of it. Finding funding has and always will be a challenge for any start-up, but having adequate financial resources is critical to your company's ongoing success. Innovative products and business models are the foundations of a promising start-up. However, you'll also need a steady flow of funds, especially in the early stages, to turn those ideas into reality.

Funding is crucial for improving technology, hiring the right people, and launching a comprehensive marketing strategy to get a foothold in the market. However, sourcing enough money to start your new venture can be difficult.

Type 1- Bootstrapping

Bootstrapping means self-funding your start-up. This option is ideal for those entrepreneurs who have just started their businesses. Getting funding can be a difficult task for first-time founders unless they show some traction and a potential business plan. Through bootstrapping, once your start-up gains some traction and builds the required confidence before exploring raising funding through investors.

Type 2 – Crowd funding Your Start-up

Crowd funding your start-up means raising funds from more than one person at the same time. In this type of funding option, more than one investor is involved. These investors offer a fixed amount of funding depending on several parameters such as your business idea, goal, financial plan of action, and plans of making money i.e. being profitable. The concept is similar to that of mutual funds on a basic level

Crowd funding can help you in multiple ways. It ensures that the start-up idea is believed by other experienced players in the ecosystem and hence it can help you raise funding right from the first stage itself i.e. at the idea stage. Since multiple stakeholders are involved crowd funding can get you the right feedback at the initial stage through different investor's perspectives.

And the best part is that you can involve common people and get your start-up funded. You can gather funds from family, friends, and budding entrepreneurs that believe in your vision and are ready to support you in your start-up journey.

Type 3 – Through Angel Investment

Angel investors are always on the lookout for promising start-ups and offer funding in exchange of convertible debt or ownership equity in the start-up. These individuals can work alone or in groups of networks to screen start-ups, share research, pool their investment capital, as well as to provide advice to their portfolio companies. Apart from offering money, angel investors can also offer mentoring and advice for your start-up.

Many companies such as Google, Yahoo & Uber are well-known examples of angel-funded firms. Raising funds through angel investors is advantageous as these investors are experienced entrepreneurs who have gone through the same phase themselves and are the ones that understand what it takes to create a billion-dollar start-up right out of an idea.

Type 4 – Through Venture Capitalists

Venture Capital (VC) is a type of start-up funding provided to small, early-stage start-ups that are emerging businesses and are deemed to have high growth potential or the ones that demonstrate high growth value (be it in terms of a number of employees, annual revenue, or both).

The firms or funds invest in early-stage start-ups for the exchange of equity, or an ownership stake, in the companies they invest in. These venture capitalists take on the risk of financing start-ups that are risky in nature in the hopes that some of the companies they support will become successful. The start-ups that attract VC funding are usually based on an innovative business model or technology and they are usually from the high technology industries, such as information technology (IT), biotechnology, or clean technology.

Typically a venture capital investment occurs after an initial "seed funding" round in Startups. The first round of institutional venture capital to fund growth is known as the Series A round. VCs provide this financing in the hopes and interest of generating a return through an eventual "exit" event. This exit can be in the form of the company selling shares to the public for the first time in an initial public offering (IPO) or undergoing a merger and acquisition (also known as a "trade sale") of the company.

Series A

In a Series, A round, VC's look for start-ups that already have a business model, and they are expected to use the money raised to increase revenue. Investments at this stage typically range from $2MM to $15MM. Some of the largest Series A VC's investing in software start-ups are New Enterprise Associates (NEA), Andreessen Horowitz, Accel Partners, Bessemer Venture Partners, Sequoia Capital, Grey croft Partners, and GGV Capital.

Series C

Series C is the third injection of investment capital. Start-ups at this stage are considered "young mature." Series C funding is often used to enable a start-up to take on a larger market share, acquire a competitor, or embark on an ambitious product development plan. Series C funding ranges from $30MM and $100MM.

Type 5 – Raise Funds through Business Incubators & Accelerators

Early stage Start-up founders that are looking to start off on the right foot can raise funds through a start-up accelerator or start-up incubator by joining their start-up programs. Start-up incubators and accelerators have a few key distinctions between them.

Accelerators "accelerate" growth of an existing company, while incubators "incubate" disruptive ideas with the hope of building out a business model and company. So, accelerators focus on scaling a business while incubators are often more focused on innovation.

If an accelerator is a greenhouse for young plants to get the optimal conditions to grow, an incubator matches quality seeds with the best soil for sprouting and growth.

Raising funds through incubators and accelerators is useful for early-stage start-ups as these options are readily available in almost every major city. The programs of Incubators and Accelerators typically run for 4-8 months of duration during which a start-up founder is introduced to various mentors, investors and other budding entrepreneurs that have enrolled for the same program.

When selecting the perfect program for their start-up, entrepreneurs should look for the right fit. Some startups may benefit from being in an incubator, whilst others may benefit from being in an accelerator.

Type 6 – Raise Funds through Bank Loans

The conventional means of taking a bank loan can also be one of the viable funding options for start-ups. However there are certain factors that the bank considers before offering you a loan. These are related to your start-up business model, expected returns, your ability to pay back the loan, management experience and expertise and last but not the least – the collateral security that will be provided by you. Under this option, entrepreneurs can raise funds through the following types of bank loans:

1. **Term Loans** – These are lent out for the purpose of buying and constructing capital assets for your business

such as machinery, plant, equipment, etc. for the use of business.

2. **Working Capital Loans** – These can be obtained for the purpose of stocking inventory or even providing credit to customers. However, banks adopt a conservative outlook while lending out money for this, and try to evaluate the working capital requirement for the start-up business based on the model and details provided.

3. **Asset Backed Loans** – Asset backed loans solve the purpose of Research &Development or marketing or expanding the start-up business. However, these are usually lent out depending upon the market value of the residential or commercial or industrial property that is to be pledged as collateral security. Usually for a period of 7-15 years banks lend approximately 70% of the assessed market value of the pledged property. In addition to this, the start-up founder will also be required to provide the bank the details of the business model as specified earlier i.e. expected returns, your ability to pay back the loan, and management experience and expertise.

Type 7 – Through the 'Start-up India' initiative

The Start-up India project by the Narendra Modi led government can be another option to raise funds for your business. As part of this initiative, the government of India has set up a **Fund of Funds** with a total corpus of Rs 10,000 crore ($1.6 billion) to empower start-ups and build a robust ecosystem by nurturing them to grow through innovation and design. This money is disbursed via the Small Industries Development Bank of India (SIDBI).

All about Start-up IDEAS: Essential Steps to Evaluating Yourself & Business Idea

Starting a business takes time and energy, and one must undergo periods of extended self-reflection to find a business idea that's both realistic and viable.

Better yet, once you have a good idea, how can you be sure it will blossom into a successful venture? These early planning stages are essential. Don't skimp on brainstorming, and put your ideas to the following test.

Start by analyzing yourself and your strengths. What interests you? What are you naturally good at?

- **What are you good at?** If you're the go-to person for certain chores or tasks, this might be a golden opportunity to turn that skill or talent into a business. However, it's important to choose something you are passionate about and can see yourself doing day in & day out.

- **What do others tell you that you're good at?** Maybe you have a hidden talent that others see in you that you never thought of as a big deal. If this is the case and that skill is something you could see yourself doing more of, it could be a great business idea.

- **What service do you wish existed that currently doesn't?** This happens all the time. You search the app store looking for something specific, thinking that it certainly exists, only to find it doesn't. This is your chance. You could pair up with an app designer or create an app yourself that could benefit people like you all over the world. Another way to think about it is what problem exists that needs a solution. Some of the most successful businesses are ones with products or services that solve problems for others.

Explore sources to spark new ideas

Sometimes you need a source of inspiration to spur that light bulb moment. Try and find inspiration in the world around you. Here are four places to look for inspiration:

- **Study successful entrepreneurs.** It's hard to know where you're going if you don't know where the great entrepreneurs before you have been. Read origin stories and study successful business titans. How did they come up with their business idea? What advice do they have to up-and-coming entrepreneurs? Learn all you can before you embark on your own journey.

- **Use your smartphone.** If you know you want to create an app, but you're not sure exactly what you want to create, search through the app store. Search categories of interest. Do you notice whether anything is missing or how apps in that category could be improved?

- **Can you find similar products or services using search engines?** The internet is incredibly helpful when it comes to finding products and services that you are in the market for. But have you ever searched and searched for something, and not been able to find it?

- **Turn to social media.** People on social media are often quick to identify issues and problems they have with current products, places, processes, etc., but few take the time to come up with a solution. Reading through people's grievances can give you great insight into problems other people have that you can solve. Online review sites can offer the same.

Identify the Need

What is the mission of your business? What is the need in the marketplace that you're filling and is it something that will appeal to a large portion of the population? Have you ever received a survey from a company asking you what you think of a product and if you would be likely to purchase the product and for how much? This is the first step in market analysis

Differentiation

What sets your company apart from the competition? If you have competitors, what will make someone choose your company over your competitor? Successful firms have a USP, or unique selling point, that serves as the foundation of the company. The more you blend in, the more you compete directly with others.

Market Analysis

Is there a sizable niche market for it?

Without a large enough market, your idea may never get off the ground. You need to determine if a niche market exists for your idea. You're better poised for success if your business improves upon what's already out there – a novel response to a recognized need.

Specifically, how big is your market? Does it include both males and females and people of all races and religions? How fast is the market growing or contracting?

It will be difficult to achieve enough market share to establish a profitable firm if you design a product or service that only appeals to a small niche market. Finding the people that make up the niche market will also necessitate a large investment in advertising.

Cost Analysis

How much will it take to open your business? If you have family obligations, you'll probably have to pay yourself, adding additional costs to your budget. How will you get the money?

Market Share

Based on your market analysis, how much of a market share do your competitors currently hold? What is left over for you or what is your strategy for taking share from them? Your business may have broad market appeal, but if the market is already saturated, the battle to gain customers may be too expensive.

Start-ups trying to manufacture new automobiles have found it exceedingly difficult to take market share from existing car companies. Evaluate whether that's a battle worth fighting and if you have the funds to fight it.

Are you passionate enough about it?

Your business will likely consume all of your time, so make sure you're passionate about it to make it successful. It's important that your idea is something you truly care about, not just something you've targeted because it seems like it could be lucrative.

Strategic Analysis Tools

These tools work by using a matrix to encourage you to think of potential internal and external factors that could affect your business.

SWOT

A SWOT analysis involves analyzing the Strengths, Weaknesses, Opportunities, and Threats for your business or idea. The articles and tools in this section will help you ask the right questions to create a useful SWOT.

PEST

A PEST analysis takes a more global strategic perspective, examining factors such as the Political, Economic, Social, and Technological climate your business will need to navigate. The more expanded version, the PESTLE, includes all of the above factors but adds on Legal and Environmental. Those are a great addition for any business considering a green business model.

Evaluating your business idea with 10 Queries

Question #1: Will this business meet a need or solve a problem?

Question #2: Is this the right time and place for this business?

Question #3: What limitations will you encounter with this business idea?

Researching your business idea

Question #4: Are there other businesses already doing what you want to do?

Question #5: Have you analysed the market?

Consider the financials of your business

Question #6: How much will this start this business?

Question #7: How will this business make money — and how long will it take?

Make sure the business fits your unique skills and experience

Question #8: Is this business something you really want to do?

Question #9: Are you capable of launching and running this business?

Question #10: How will you feel if things don't go according to plan?

The Bottom Line

Stop talking and start writing. Talking about an idea prior to doing some initial processing on paper tricks our brains into thinking that we are actually doing something about the concept

As an entrepreneur, your dream is likely centered on being one of those $1 billion or more businesses, but remember that many businesses fail and that's largely due to poor planning. Before investing a large amount of money in your business idea, create a plan and make sure that your idea is something that customers would be excited about purchasing. There are plenty of great opportunities waiting for a small business owner who follows a business start-up system

Intellectual Property Rights, critical for the success of startups

When entrepreneurs begin on their unique business idea, they have no doubt that their idea would be a commercial success in the market; their main focus is initially to start giving the appearance to the venture.

In the middle of so many different things that go into starting and building a startup from a single idea, the word 'Intellectual Property' (IP) is generally not just their main focus. And even if they think about IP protection, it seems to be too costly for a startup to work on.

Entrepreneurs must understand that evaluating IP implications is not just about protecting the work you are doing but, it is also very essential to check whether someone else has an IP for the same work. Very often, there could be people in different parts of the world working on the same idea

Intellectual Property Rights prevent opponents, bigger establishments/ companies from stealing/ copying indications, inventions, brand names/trademarks, which in twist furnishes start-ups to broaden and make profits with exclusivity for a set period. Further, there is invariably a high probability of delivering enthusiasm to investors, clients, and other stakeholders, for start-ups who have patented their core creations and registered their brand name/ trademark; since it indicates high standards and "viability study" performed by the Start-ups.

Start-ups, due to their insufficient resources, cannot opt to avail themselves of the comprehensive IPR protection. Therefore, the start-ups, depending upon their industries and enterprise, must analyze and prioritize their Intellectual Property Rights, wherein such IP Rights play a significant role and sometimes happen to be the only accessible investments with a start-up. Failure to perform the same might create an obstacle to the smooth functioning of the enterprise particularly between the founders of the Start-up, promoters, negotiations with the existing and future investors, or while quitting the business.

In today's competitive and fast-growing environment, IP can be a Unique Selling Proposition (USP) of the goods or services which will help to create a sustainable and protective differentiator for the company.

By owning an IP, it creates a high obstruction, thereby helping you to develop your venture faster and more efficiently. IP always has a high weight for the investors. Therefore, it creates a good reputation for your venture. Moreover, IP identifies as the main ingredient for startups around the world to get a competitive benefit in the market.

There are three significant ways in which a startup can protect its intellectual property:

1) Patents
2) Trademarks
3) Copyrights

Intellectual property is an asset for it's the creator and has a commercial value with it. If IP is correctly and strategically conserve then it can take the valuation of a company to a completely another level.

IPR yields you the following advantages

1. Can sell or license for creating an additional revenue stream.

2. Offering distinctive products/services to your customers.

3. It can become an essential part of your marketing or branding (Exclusivity).

4. Intellectual properties are assets that you can use as security against loans.

5. Start-ups can legally protect your Intellectual property in the following manners:

1. Copyrights

Certain protection is automatically granted to the author for their original, creative or intellectual work. Know more about copyright registration in India to ensure taking correct steps in the right direction.

Works include; Books, lectures, dramatic and musical works, cinematography, drawings, paintings, architecture, sculpture, photographs, illustrations, maps, plans sketches etc.

Rights: To distribute copies of the work to the public by sale or other transfer of ownership, or by rental, lease, or lending and to perform the work publicly in person or through an audio transmission.

Validity: It is not mandatory to register but is highly recommended. The validity of copyright lasts the lifetime of the author and even till the 60 years after his/her death. The owner is given protection in most countries.

2. Trademarks

Trademark: At first, register trademark online as this acts as a brand element distinguishing your goods and services from those of your competitors and other traders in the market. It creates a distinct identity for your company and thereby securing a brand from being counterfeited.

Marks: Word mark, a logo mark or a slogan, shapes, and unconventional marks like colours, sounds, gestures, animation, holograms etc. can be registered under trademark.

Rights: Gives the exclusive right to use the mark and prevent anyone from using it without permission. The owner also enjoys the right to license, assign and sell the mark in return of compensation.

Validity: 10 years which can be made perpetual, as along as renewed every 10 years. Should be applied separately in every country in which protection is required and has a market in.

3. Patents

Patents come to play when you are looking to protect a new invention that is original and can be used to simplify the lives of people.

Condition: Patent requires an idea to be novel and unique. The industrial procedures can be patented especially if a non-obvious step is introduced in it.

Rights: It gives an exclusive authority over the patented invention, the right to exclude others and exploit the patent and earn from it.

Validity: Patent protection is a territorial right and therefore it is effective only within the territory of India (or the country where applied). Separate patents required to be filed for each country where the protection is required. A patent is valid for a period of 20 years after which it goes in the public domain.

It is best to consider IP as something that offers an additive advantage that is beyond the concept of making money or even branding for that matter. It is something with which the business esteem is connected. Insuring the intellectual property is also a common norm since it is an asset. One of the quintessential business components is to have IP protection a part of budgeting and business plan as well.

Protecting Intellectual Property against any sort of infringement by others.

1. You can defend it in the court of law to claim your sole right on it.
2. Can legally stop others to use, make, sell or import without your agreement.
3. You can earn royalties by licensing it or make money selling it.
4. Use your trademark for strategic alliances.

Start-up Valuation can be made on the Basis of IP Rights

New companies don't really have monstrous products' stocks or workforce to begin with. Subsequently, a large portion of the estimation of a start-up, for the most part, gets from their IP rights. It has been assessed that on the normal, over 80% of the estimation of a new business depends on their IP portfolio. Protecting your IPR is the best and the only way that helps you to create a sustainable and defensible differentiator in a highly competitive market.

Women Entrepreneurs for Building Strong Economy

Entrepreneurship is one of the most important element necessary to build the economy. Every nation tries to improve economic growth for prosperity and better life standard of its people, and entrepreneur is a catalytic agent of change. In the past few decades, the role of women in our society has changed drastically and for the better. Women are now encouraged to occupy the corporate positions. The gender stereotypes which were more prevalent in the society decades ago are slowly getting dissolved. Women bring a different set of perspectives to problem solving that can enhance the quality of the solution at large. The unique set of issues and experiences that women put forth helps in quality decision making.

In Indian scenario, it is not a cake walk for a women to take any decision independently. She has to face many problems in carrying out any economic activities or undertaking any entrepreneurial task. She has to undergo various socioeconomic and other problems as entrepreneur as they are not treated equally to men due to social and cultural traditions.

In this golden age of globalization, digitalization, and start-up booms, India is seeing a revolution about women entrepreneurs. Today's women entrepreneurs do not come only from the established business families or the higher-income sections of the population, they come from all walks of life and all parts of the country.

Now in recent India, it is observed that there has been an increasing trend in the number of women-owned enterprises as the result of drastic changes in the present world. Women are participating in large numbers in the present world of business. Women are successful in multiple professions like law, science, medicine, aeronautics, space exploration, and even police and military services, they are showing their interest even in business and industry. They have proved that they are no less them men in efficiency, hard work, or intelligence, provided they are given proper scope.

Researchers contend that women business owners possess certain specific characteristics that promote their creativity and generate new ideas and ways of doing things. Women entrepreneurs tend to be highly motivated & self-directed; they also exhibit a high internal locus of control & achievement. Women entrepreneurs have the unique tendency to build and maintain long-term relationships. They have more effective communication, organizational, and networking skills than their male counterparts.

According to studies, it has been observed that Women are very good entrepreneurs as they can maintain a workable balance in life. These factors may vary from place to place and business to business but women entrepreneurship is necessary for the growth of any economy whether it is large or small.

Significance of Women in India's Entrepreneurial Sector

Indian women have been at the receiving end of criticism but much to the dismay of their sceptics, they have mostly appeared triumphant as the dust of criticism settled. The industry has much to gain and nothing to lose with women in business. The merits are innumerable.

- Indian industry's think-tank gets bigger.

- New opportunities are created.

- More employment opportunities are generated.

- Per-capita income increases.

- Indians enjoy a better standard of living.

- Education and awareness become common.

- Future becomes brighter for the next generation.

- Women gain a better understanding of managing family and business concurrently.

- Indian women achieve a sense of self-realization and self-fulfillment.

- Women gain a better ability to take risks and business decisions.

- Women become more confident.

Highly educated, technically sound, and professionally qualified women must be encouraged for managing their own businesses, rather than being employed in any outlets. The uncultivated talents of young women can be identified, trained, and exploited for various types of industries to increase productivity in the industrial sector as well as the nation

Opportunities for Indian Women Entrepreneurs

Educated, gifted, and qualified females can enter virtually any business. Successful women have been representing and continue to represent brands like Times of India, PepsiCo, ICICI, TAFE, HP, HSBC, and J.P Morgan along with other names. The list in the lines to come puts forward a few sectors where women entrepreneurs of India can excel as senior managers and owners.

- Eco-friendly/ Bio-friendly sectors

- IT sector

- Event Management
- Lifestyle sector
- Beauty and cosmetic
- Healthcare
- Travel and tourism sector
- Food, food processing, and beverages
- Telecommunications
- Financing
- Plastic manufacturing
- Local and international trading
- Property and estate

Factors Driving Women to Start Businesses or Join Workforce

Women entrepreneurs are empowering 50% of India's start-up ecosystem, driven by:

- **Recognition**: Recognition in the form of admiration, regard, esteem, and renown motivates women entrepreneurs. According to a survey by Bain & Company, more than 45% of Indian women in rural areas were driven to start a business for gaining recognition.

- **Results**: Women-led start-ups provide 35% higher ROI compared to those led by men. This ability to generate more returns encourages women to start their own businesses.

- **Fulfilling unmet needs**: The inherent need in women to provide for the family is a key factor. As they make 85% of purchase decisions, the need to provide a better lifestyle motivates women.

- **Education**: India ranks among the top worldwide for producing female graduates in the science, technology, engineering, and mathematics (STEM) industry, with as many as 40% of women graduating from this field. Indian women are game-changers in the fields of science and technology.

Fortunately, recognizing the significance of the socioeconomic contributions of women entrepreneurs from semi-urban and rural regions, the government has brought forth several schemes and policies to enable women to start their own enterprises. Some of these include the National Mission for Empowerment of Women, the Prime Minister's Rojgar Yojana (PMRY), Entrepreneurial Development Programmes (EDPs), Management Development Programmes, and Women's Development Corporations (WDC).

Government Initiatives to Encourage Women's Participation

The Indian government has increased the budget for Women and Child Development by 14% in 2021. It has set aside over Rs. 30,000 crores (US$ 3.97 billion) in FY21. This budgetary allocation also includes various development schemes as listed below.

- **Bharatiya Mahila Bank Business Loan**: This type of business loan was set up in 2017 to help women access cheap loans and dream big despite their lack of resources. The scheme provides loans of over Rs. 20 crores (US$ 2.46 million) for women entrepreneurs. A collateral-free loan can also be availed of for loans worth less than Rs. 1 crore (US$ 0.13 million).

- **Dena Shakti Scheme**: This scheme was launched for women entrepreneurs looking to start their business in certain sectors such as agriculture, retail, and manufacturing. The scheme provides loans at an interest rate that is 0.25% below the base rate. The maximum loan application is Rs. 20 lakhs (US$ 26,468).

- **Udyogini Scheme**: This scheme is for women with an annual income of Rs. 1.5 lakh (US$ 1,985). It provides loans of up to Rs. 3 lakh (US$ 3,890) for women wanting to start a business but having no capital.

- **Women Entrepreneurship Platform**: This is a flagship platform started by NITI Aayog to promote women's entrepreneurship. The platform hosts various workshops and educational events to motivate women to start their own businesses.

- **Pradhan Mantri Mudra Yojana**: Even though the scheme was started to help anyone looking to set up a micro/small enterprise get an institutional credit of up to Rs. 10 lakhs (US$ 13,240), it was mostly availed of by women.

It is estimated that over 30 million more women-owned businesses are expected to provide 150–170 million jobs by 2030. This could be a game changer and help the economic outlook look brighter than ever.

National start-up Day and its Significance

"The start-up India initiative by the Indian Government in 2016 has catalyzed the start-up ecosystem and has resulted that India is now "World's 3rd Largest start-up Ecosystem" over 61000 recognized start-ups. And, the day when this initiative took place is now known as the National start-up Day."

India is recognized as a start-up hub and such initiatives encourage innovation across sectors. January 16 is marked as National start-up day with a motto to encourage the spirit of entrepreneurship and promote achievements of Indian start-ups. It is also commemorated to provide a platform for start-up entrepreneurs to discuss innovation for India's youth and their contribution to the economy. The motive behind encouraging the idea of entrepreneurship is to give a boost to schemes like Make-in-India. India has emerged as one of the largest hub for young start-ups, given its massive youth population in the past few years and a vibrant consumption economy there is an opportunity to experiment and solve problems differently.

So, if thinking about starting your own business, remember that it's not just about the destination, it's about the journey. Embrace the adventure and enjoy the ride. The biggest adventure one can ever take is to realize the dream of creating jobs.

It is most important that, Entrepreneurs and start-up founders need stay true to their passion and not to settle for anything less than their best work. Finding our true inner voice and pursuing it with love and dedication is the key to success and fulfilment.

Currently, start-ups are contributing about 3% to the overall GDP and that is likely to become 10% in the next one decade and this gives us even more confidence in working towards creating proper infrastructure to fuel the growth of early stage start-ups and those entrepreneurs building in the Bharat. Tier 2,3 city based start-ups contribute about 50% to the National data on start-ups, since the last three years we have been consistently seeing a spike in the proportion of start-ups applying to us for funding. In 2022, we had almost 30% of the start-ups coming from towns beyond the metros.

National start-up Day is a great testimony as well as inspiration for all the stakeholders of the Indian start-up ecosystem - Entrepreneurs, Start-ups, their employees, VCs and angel investors. The current government has taken some quick and prudent steps to promote entrepreneurship and make start-ups as the "backbone" of our economy.

New designs, innovations and ideas are constantly emerging and the audience is more open than ever to embracing local, home-grown start-ups. Together, we are growing as a unit and propelling the future of entrepreneurship."

The celebration of National Start-Up Day was the icing on the cake. This gave a boost to entrepreneurs, which accelerated the foundation of 69,000 start-ups last year. We, as a start-up, have received tremendous support in terms of new scheme launches and smoother regulations for a stronger future."

It is also marked to promote the importance of start-up initiatives and make them a part of the mainstream. Encouraging youth to take up entrepreneurship as a primary career option is also an agenda behind this initiative.

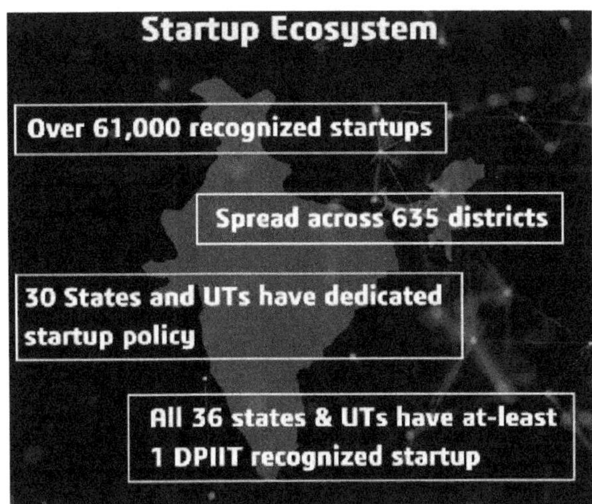

"The declaration of 16 January as the National start-up Day has been a truly inspiring initiative for the Indian start-up sector.

REVA NEST- TBI is established to nurture and handhold start-ups and support aspiring entrepreneurs. On the occasion of National start-up day Student, Alumni and External start-up Entrepreneurs participated with enthusiasm and shared their experience as a start-up. Start-up is all about learning curve mentioned by one the CEO. India is set to play an important role in the global economy. And one of the pillars of this growth will be our home grown start-ups and Universities are playing vital role through Technology business incubators to enable and support start-up ecosystem.